DISASTERS!

Experiment Log

Wow! It's Windy, Wet, and Wild!

by Susan Wright

SCHOLASTIC INC

New York Toronto London Auckland Sydney Mexico City New Delhi Hong Kong

Design by Paula Jo Smith
Cover, Parrot, Luis, Prescott, and Alberta illustrations by Sam Ward
Instructional illustrations by Daniel Aycock

12 11 10 9 8 7 6 5 4 3 2 1   1 2 3 4 5 6/0

Printed in the U.S.A.
First Scholastic printing, January 2001

TABLE OF CONTENTS

Introduction......................Page 6

The Experiments:

#1 High Impact!...................Page 8

#2 Fiery Mountain................Page 13

#3 Live Lava.....................Page 17

#4 A Slippery Slope..............Page 21

#5 There She Blows!..............Page 24

#6 The Eye of the Storm..........Page 28

#7 Terrible Twisters.............Page 33

#8 Flash Flood!..................Page 36

#9 An Earthshaking Experience....Page 41

#10 Earthquake Survival Structure Page 44

Sneak Peek Puzzle................Page 48

INTRODUCTION

Hi! Prescott Forester III here. Alberta Wong, Luis Antilla, and I have been having fun with these excellent experiments in the science lab at Einstein Elementary. We're lucky enough to be the lab assistants of Mr. Ethan Flask, so we get to be the first to try the experiments! If you've already read Watch Out! you know we've been studying natural disasters. They're just like the disasters that you hear about on the news— things like hurricanes, tornadoes, and earthquakes. Now you can try these way cool Disasters! experiments, too!

The neat thing about natural disasters is that scientists haven't figured them all out yet. So you can be a real scientist and make your own hypotheses and observations about storms and stuff!

In this book, you'll get to make your own volcano, cause an avalanche and a flood, see a tornado, create a hurricane, and more! So get ready for disaster to strike—of your own making, that is!

—Prescott

7

#1: HIGH IMPACT!

Have you ever wondered what happened to all the dinosaurs? I did, until Mr. Flask explained there is a theory that a massive meteorite hit the earth more than 65 million years ago and that some scientists think the impact destroyed all those big beasts! With this neat experiment, you can make your own meteorite craters. But don't throw your meteorite too hard, or you could have a bigger mess on your hands than mass extinction!

HERE'S THE OTHER STUFF YOU'LL NEED:

A plastic container (like a square or rectangular Tupperware® container)

Flour (enough for a 1-inch [2.5-cm] layer in the container—about 2 to 3 cups [500-700 mL])

Newspaper or colored construction paper

from your DISASTERS! KIT go grab:

Meteorite ball

NOTE: This experiment can be messy. It's a good idea to do it outside!

READY, SET, SCIENCE!

STEP 1   Spread layers of newspaper or colored construction paper on the floor in an area that's just about 2 feet (1 meter) square.

STEP 2   Put the flour in the plastic container so that you have a layer about 1 inch (2.5 cm) deep. Lightly shake the container to make a nice flat surface. Place the container with the flour in the middle of the square of newspaper or construction paper.

STEP 3   Stand in front of the container, holding the meteorite ball at about waist height. Now, let go of your meteorite ball (drop it, don't throw it!) so that it hits the flour. Carefully remove the meteorite ball from the flour, and you can see the impact crater that it made in the flour! Look at the crater, and record your observations in *RAPID DISASTER RESPONSE*. Drop the meteorite ball into the flour again. What happens to the first crater when a new crater is formed? Record your observations in *RAPID DISASTER RESPONSE*.

QUICK TIP

Drop, DON'T throw, your meteorite ball. You'll get better craters!

STEP 3

STEP 4   Shake or "resurface" the container, so that you can make some new craters. Experiment by dropping the meteorite ball from different heights to see what happens.

First, take the meteorite ball and drop it from knee height into the flour. Second, hold the meteorite ball above your head to drop it into the flour. Record your observations in *RAPID DISASTER RESPONSE*.

> Why did the dinosaur cross the road?
> Because the chicken hadn't evolved yet!

OBSERVATIONS

What does the flour look like after the meteorite hits in **STEP 3**?

What happens to the first crater in **STEP 3** when a new crater is formed?

Where does the flour land in **STEP 3** when you drop the meteorite ball from waist height—in the container or on the newspaper/construction paper?

Where does the flour land in **STEP 4** when you drop the meteorite ball from knee height? From over your head?

Draw the shapes of the craters you get when you drop the meteorite ball from different heights:

1. WAIST HEIGHT   **2. KNEE HEIGHT**   **3. OVER YOUR HEAD**

Dig those Funky Meteorite Craters

A meteor is a metallic rock that flies through space. When it smacks into a planet, it's called a meteorite. Just like the craters you make in this experiment, the impact of a meteorite leaves behind a round hole or crater. The explosion can throw rock debris very far away, forming streaks that are called rays. Your meteorite makes rays, too, when the streaks of flour land on the newspaper or colored construction paper! The second time you drop the meteorite ball, the flour rays from this second crater start to fill the first crater. And when you drop the meteorite ball from higher up, you get a deeper crater and better rays, too, because the ball's hitting the flour harder.

Some scientists think that when a massive meteorite hit the earth 65 million years ago, so much rock debris was thrown into the air that it blocked the warmth of the sun, changing the tropical climate to a wintry one. It's thought that most of the dinos died because they couldn't survive the cold weather!

GO GRAB a skinny rubber band. Use it to slingshot your meteorite into the flour at top speed! What happens to the flour now? Record your observations in **RAPID DISASTER RESPONSE**.

NOTE: This experiment can be really messy! You might want to stay outside for this one, too.

RAPID DISASTER RESPONSE
OBSERVATIONS

How does throwing (slingshotting), not dropping, the meteorite ball change the size and shape of the crater?

How does throwing the meteorite ball change the size and shape of the rays of flour?

High-Speed Meteorite! Happenings

Real meteorite craters are always circular. It doesn't matter how fast the meteorite is going or if it hits the ground at a steep angle. That's 'cause the impact of the meteorite creates a shock wave that spreads out in a circle, exploding the rock! Just like your craters, the depth of real meteorite craters depend on three things: 1. how big the meteorite is, 2. how fast the meteorite is traveling, and 3. the density of the ground where the meteorite hits (you'll check this out in **EXPERIMENT WITH THE EXPERIMENT 2** that follows). When the impact explosion is really tremendous, the crater is super-deep, and a larger amount of exploded rock debris is thrown from the crater to form rays!

P.S. The atmosphere of the earth (that's all the air and clouds and stuff) slows meteorites down so that they all hit at more or less the same speed (and that's still pretty fast). But the moon has no atmosphere, so meteorites can hit its surface at all different speeds.

Pour out the flour, and fill your container with different stuff to try this experiment again. You can use sugar, sand, cornmeal, or even powdered drink mix to see how a different surface affects the meteorite crater. Drop your meteorite ball into the container a few times to see how it changes the cratered surface.

Facts About Impacts on Other Worlds

This experiment shows you how changing the density of the surface affects the size and shape of the craters. I bet that when you used flour you got deeper craters than when you used cornmeal, sugar, sand, or drink mix. Cornmeal, sugar, sand, and drink mix are denser than flour—that is, a cup of each of these substances weighs more than flour does. So they make shallower craters. Also, cornmeal, sugar, sand, and drink mix have fairly large grains compared to powdered flour. These grains slip against one another easily, making the craters slump. This is kind of like the way meteorite craters on Earth erode because of rain and wind. The moon, on the other hand, has no rain or wind—and its dusty surface makes perfect craters, just like the flour in your first experiment. That's why it's easier to see craters on the moon than on Earth. Just go outside when there's a full moon, and you can see dozens of real meteorite craters for yourself!

What do you do when there's a blue moon?

Cheer it up! Try to

#2: FIERY MOUNTAIN

I've always wanted to see a volcano erupt, but there haven't been any volcanoes near Einstein Elementary...until now! Here's your chance to make your own volcano and watch it erupt. Why don't you try it? Trust me—it's a blast!

from your DISASTERS! KIT go grab:

The Mad Science Volcano Kit, which contains:

A paper semicircle

Papier-maché mix

Newsprint

A little paper cup

Brown paint

A paintbrush

Orange food coloring powder

HERE'S THE OTHER STUFF YOU'LL NEED:

2 feet (60 cm) of plastic wrap or aluminum foil

Tape

Scissors

A small bowl

A fork

A pie tin or cookie sheet

Measuring cup

Vinegar

Water

Baking soda

NOTE: This experiment takes two days to do. On the first day, you make your volcano. On the next, you paint the volcano and make it erupt!

EXPERIMENT CONTINUES ON THE NEXT PAGE!

READY, SET, SCIENCE!

STEP 1 Use the sheet of plastic wrap or aluminum foil to cover the table or counter where you're working.

STEP 2 To make the shape of the volcano, tape the ends of the paper semicircle together. Place the little paper cup in the small opening of the cone. If the cup doesn't fit, retape the paper semicircle to fit around the cup.

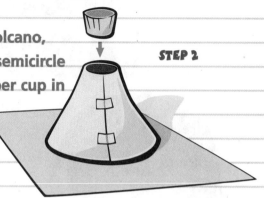

STEP 2

STEP 3 Cut the newsprint into strips approximately 1 inch by 3 inches (2.5 cm x 8 cm).

STEP 4 Open the bag of papier-maché mix and pour it into the small bowl. Add one-half cup (125 mL) of water. Mix together, using the fork, until the papier-maché turns into a paste.

STEP 5

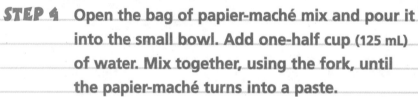

STEP 5 Dip a strip of newsprint into the papier-maché. Make sure you completely coat each strip! Wipe the extra mix from the strip, using your fingers.

STEP 6 Place the strip of newsprint on the volcano, and smooth down the edges.

STEP 7 Repeat steps 5 and 6 until the volcano is covered with papier-maché strips. Then let the volcano dry overnight. Real volcanoes aren't smooth, so it's okay for your volcano to be lumpy!

STEP 7

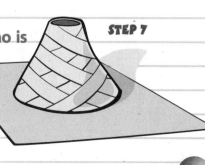

STEP 8 When the papier-maché on your volcano is dry the next day, paint it with the brown paint. Wait about 30 minutes for the paint to dry. Then go on to step 9.

STEP 9 Place your volcano on the pie tin or cookie sheet.

STEP 10 Measure one quarter-cup (60 mL) of baking soda, and dump it into the small paper cup in the top of your volcano. Add all of the orange food coloring powder to the paper cup and mix the baking soda and the food coloring powder together with your finger.

STEP 10

QUICK TIP

Just to play it safe, you might do this part of the experiment over the sink or outside.

STEP 11 Now very slowly pour one half-cup (125 mL) of vinegar to the small paper cup. Stand back, watch what happens, and record your observations in **RAPID DISASTER RESPONSE**.

How do you know when a volcano is angry?

When it blows its top!

RAPID DISASTER RESPONSE

OBSERVATIONS

What happens to the baking soda and orange food coloring powder when the vinegar is poured into the volcano in **STEP 11**?

CONCLUSION

Why do you think the baking soda, food coloring powder, and vinegar bubble out of the volcano?

Chillin' with the Fiery Mountain

When you mix baking soda and vinegar together, you make a chemical reaction that creates a gas called *carbon dioxide* (the same gas that's inside soda bubbles). It's that chemical reaction that causes your volcano to erupt! (The food coloring powder just makes the reaction look neat.) The carbon dioxide gas expands really fast, and your fizzy lava comes spilling over the sides of your volcano!

A real volcano has lots of gases and *lava* (hot molten rock) inside. Most of the time, the gas and the lava can escape gradually through a vent, or hole, in the volcano. Sometimes extra-thick lava clogs up the hole. The pressure builds up from the gas inside, until—*ka-blam!* Eruption time! Lava shoots out of the volcano, just like the fizzy stuff that comes out of your volcano!

#3: LIVE LAVA

I went to Hawaii on my summer vacation, and the coolest thing I saw was the Kilauea Volcano. It started erupting before I was born, way back in 1983, and believe it or not, lava is still flowing out! I actually stood on one lava flow that once covered a whole town! In this experiment, you'll see what happens when lava takes over your kitchen (well, sort of)!

from your DISASTERS! KIT go grab:

2 mini houses

from your MAD LAB PACK go grab:

The measuring scoop

HERE'S THE OTHER STUFF YOU'LL NEED:

Ketchup

Maple syrup

A cookie sheet

Paper towels

EXPERIMENT CONTINUES ON THE NEXT PAGE!

READY, SET, SCIENCE!

STEP 1 Put the cookie sheet down on the counter or a table so that one of the longer sides is closest to you. You're going to have a race between ketchup and maple syrup!

STEP 2 Place one mini house against each long side of the cookie sheet (that's two houses total). You'll have a better race if you put the houses halfway down the long sides, next to each edge. Lift the cookie sheet, and use a tiny smear of maple syrup to keep the houses in place.

STEP 2

STEP 3 Use the scoop to pour 3 tablespoons of maple syrup in the left corner of the long side of the cookie sheet (the side with the red house in the picture on this page). Then use the scoop to dump out 3 tablespoons of ketchup in the other left corner of the long side of the cookie sheet (the side with the yellow house in the picture on this page).

STEP 3

STEP 4 Carefully lift the end of the cookie sheet that has the puddles of liquid. Watch the maple syrup and ketchup slide to the other end of the cookie sheet. Which liquid gets to its house first? Which liquid pushes its house farther? Record your observations in *RAPID DISASTER RESPONSE*.

STEP 4

RAPID DISASTER RESPONSE

HYPOTHESES

Which liquid do you think will reach its house first, maple syrup or ketchup?

Which liquid do you think will push its house farther, maple syrup or ketchup?

OBSERVATIONS

Which liquid is thicker, maple syrup or ketchup?

Which liquid actually reaches its house first in **STEP 4**, maple syrup or ketchup?

Which liquid actually pushes its house farther in **STEP 4**, maple syrup or ketchup?

CONCLUSIONS

When a volcano erupts, which kind of lava do you think flows out of the volcano more quickly, thick or thin lava?

Which kind of lava do you think would cause more destruction in the area surrounding the volcano, thick or thin lava?

Lava rocks!

Getting into the Flow
(with Lava)

The kitchen stuff you used in this experiment imitates lava. Some lava is very thick (like the ketchup in this experiment) and can push a whole house over, while other lava is thinner (like the maple syrup) and moves much faster. The thinner lava flows like a river, zooming through the lowest channel it can find down the side of the volcano. Sometimes this lava will flow down a riverbed or valley, going around towns and houses. But the thicker lava can move in a mass of rock hundreds of feet (or meters) wide, mowing down everything in its path!

Lava comes from rock that melts deep beneath the surface of the earth, with temperatures ranging from about 1,300° F to 2,200° F (700° C to 1200° C). When a volcano keeps erupting, layers of lava rock can build up really fast! That's how some mountains got to be so tall, like Mount Saint Helens in Washington and Mount Fuji in Japan—they're really volcanoes!

A volcano that doesn't erupt lava for a long time is *dormant* (that means sleeping). But don't be fooled—a sleepy volcano can wake up again with hardly any warning (even years later)!

EXPERIMENT WITH THE EXPERIMENT: YUMMY LAVA!

GO GRAB some taffy, and put it in the hot sun or hold it in the palm of your hand for a few minutes. When it starts to melt, it stretches and bends more easily. You can probably stretch it pretty far before the taffy breaks. Now cool the taffy by putting it in the refrigerator or freezer. After a few minutes, take the taffy out. Try stretching the stuff—is it easier or harder to stretch? When the taffy gets cold, it gets hard. That's also how lava works. When lava is hot, it flows. As it cools, it turns back into solid rock!

#4: A SLIPPERY SLOPE

When Mr. Flask taught our class about avalanches and how they happen, I thought it was pretty wild. I kept thinking about snowboarding. Have you ever been? It's great! You can really whip down the mountain, sort of like riding a skateboard down a steep slope, but you keep going for a long time.

I didn't realize how dangerous snow and ice can be when they start moving. Check out this experiment, and see if you can cause an avalanche of your own!

from your DISASTERS! KIT go grab:

Dried peas

HERE'S THE OTHER STUFF YOU'LL NEED:

1 heavy metal teaspoon

3 books

READY, SET, SCIENCE!

STEP 1   Hold the spoon in one hand, and see how many dried peas you can stack on it. Count each pea as you place it on the stack. How many peas can you place on the spoon before a bunch of them fall off? Record your observations in *RAPID DISASTER RESPONSE*.

STEP 2   Now, lay one book flat on a table. Put one of the other books down, with one end on the first book and the other end on the table, so it's slanted. Put the spoon on the slanted book with the handle pointing downward.

STEP 2

STEP 3   Count the peas as you carefully place them in the bowl of the spoon. How many peas can you stack *this time* before the peas slide off? Record your observations in *RAPID DISASTER RESPONSE*.

STEP 4   Now, repeat this experiment, but this time make the slant even steeper. Stack *two* books on top of each other, then place the third book at a slant, with one end on the stacked books and the other end resting on the table. Put the spoon on the slanted book, with the handle pointing downward.

STEP 4

How do you spell hard water with only three letters?

I-C-E.

STEP 5   Count the peas as you carefully place them in the bowl of the spoon. How many can you stack *this time* before the peas slide off? Record your observations in *RAPID DISASTER RESPONSE*.

OBSERVATIONS

How many peas can you stack when you're holding the spoon in **STEP 1**?

How many peas can you stack in the spoon slanted on the one book in **STEP 3**?

When the peas fall off the spoon in **STEP 3**, do they come from the bottom or the top layer of peas?

How many peas can you stack on the spoon slanted on the two books in **STEP 5**?

When the peas fall off the spoon in **STEP 5**, do they come from the bottom or the top layer of peas?

CONCLUSIONS:

Why do you think you can stack more peas on the spoon in **STEP 1** than you can in **STEP 3**? Why do you think you can stack more peas on the spoon in **STEP 3** than you can in **STEP 5**?

Here's Why What Goes Up Must Come Down!

In this experiment, the spoon creates a model of interlocking ice crystals in snow, holding the peas in place just like the curve of a mountainside or crevice holds a pack of snow in place. But your pile of peas isn't too stable—if you add too many peas to the spoon or if your hand shakes a little as you hold the spoon, that's enough to destroy the balance of your pea pile, and whoops! some peas fall off your spoon.

The same thing happens in an avalanche: Some teeny change occurs to a large, delicately balanced mass of rock or snow, causing it to move down the mountain slope and sweep up everything in its path. Usually avalanches are set off by things like temperature changes, sudden vibrations, or even very loud noises such as gunshots. The steeper the slope, the smaller the trigger is needed to get things moving. So the more you slant your spoon, the fewer peas you can stack on it.

Probably your pea avalanches start when the bottom layer of peas collapses. Most real avalanches happen when the bottom layers of snow start to slide after repeatedly being melted (from the enormous pressure of snow pressing down on top) and then refrozen.

Avalanches are real speed demons—they can move faster than 100 miles (160 kph) per hour, burying anything in their path. They are so dangerous that in many ski areas avalanche patrols use explosives to set off controlled avalanches!

#5: THERE SHE BLOWS!

You probably know that all hurricanes have names. The National Hurricane Service used to name all hurricanes after girls (for example, Hurricane Gloria), but now boys also get to have hurricanes named after them (for example, Hurricane Andrew). You can make a hurricane of your own with this experiment—it blew _me_ away!

from your DISASTERS! KIT go grab:

2 mini houses
2 mini cars

HERE'S THE OTHER STUFF YOU'LL NEED:

A cylindrical cardboard container (An empty oatmeal container works great! You can also use a plastic peanut butter jar or a foil-lined chip container.)

A balloon

A rubber band

Scissors

A sharpened pencil

Flour

A cookie sheet

Newspaper

A large spoon

A ruler

NOTE: This experiment isn't very messy, but you'll need to make a pile of flour, so you might want to hang out in the kitchen or go outside to do this one. That will make cleanup easier!

READY, SET, SCIENCE!

STEP 1 Your cylindrical container should have one large open end and one closed end. Use the pencil to punch a small pencil-sized hole in the center of the closed end.

NOTE: If you use a plastic cylindrical container (like a peanut butter jar) or a foil-lined cylindrical container (like a potato chip tube), get an adult to help you punch the hole.

STEP 2

STEP 2 Cut the neck off the balloon, leaving only the wide part of the balloon. Pull the balloon over the open end of the cylindrical container until the rubber is stretched tight.

STEP 3 While holding the balloon on the container, put the rubber band around it to keep it in place.

STEP 3

STEP 4 Spread the newspaper on the table or floor, then put the cookie sheet in the middle. Use the spoon to make a pile of flour on the cookie sheet approximately 3 inches (8 cm) high. That's your hill. Place the houses and cars on the top of the hill.

What's yours, but everybody uses it more than you do?

your name!

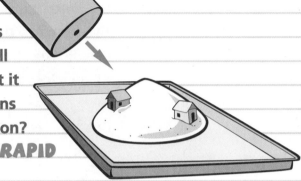

STEP 5 Carefully aim the container's small hole at the flour hill, holding it about 6 inches (15 cm) away from the hill. Pull gently on the balloon and let it go with a snap! What happens when you let go of the balloon? Record your observations in *RAPID DISASTER RESPONSE*.

STEP 6 Experiment by moving the cylindrical container closer to or farther away from the flour hill with the houses and cars. Try holding the container 4 inches (10 cm) or 2 inches (5 cm) away from the houses on the hill. Use the ruler to measure how far the flour blows, depending on how close you are, and record your observations in *RAPID DISASTER RESPONSE*.

STEP 7 Now try this experiment using a stream of running water. Turn on the sink faucet (or water hose, if you're outside) halfway, until a stream of water is running out. Then aim the small hole in your cylindrical container at the water, and snap the balloon. Move the container closer to the water and snap the balloon; then try pulling the container farther away while you snap the balloon. Record your observations and conclusions in *RAPID DISASTER RESPONSE*.

What runs but never walks?

Water!

RAPID DISASTER RESPONSE

OBSERVATIONS

What happens to the flour hill, houses, and cars when the balloon is snapped in **STEP 5**?

How far does the flour blow in **STEPS 5 AND 6**:
When the container is 6 inches (15 cm) from the hill?
When the container is 4 inches (10 cm) from the hill?
When the container is 2 inches (5 cm) from the hill?

What happens to the water in **STEP 7** when you snap the balloon on the cylindrical container?

CONCLUSIONS

Why do you think the wind from the small hole in your cylindrical container is so strong?

What do you think can happen to real houses and cars when they're hit by the strong winds of a hurricane?

The Real Deal on High Winds

When you snap the balloon on your cylindrical container, the air inside is suddenly squeezed or compressed. That forces it out the small hole at the other end, and the air comes out quickly and moves with a spiral motion. That's what a hurricane is—strong winds zooming around in a fast, spiral motion!

In this experiment, the closer the container is to the houses and flour hill, the stronger the wind, blowing away the flour and knocking over the houses. The closer a real hurricane is to an object (like a house), the more damage it does to that object. The wind from the container is also strong enough to make the flow of water jump, just like the way a real strong wind can blow rain so that it falls at a slant rather than straight down from the sky!

#6: THE EYE OF THE STORM

I visited my aunt and uncle in Florida last year, and we got hit by a hurricane! The wind was blowing at 100 miles (160 km) an hour, and rain was coming down in buckets. Suddenly, the wind and rain totally stopped, as if the storm had never happened at all. My uncle took me outside so I could see the <u>eye of the storm.</u> It was just the weirdest thing: The sky was blue, like it was a perfect summer day! Then about 20 minutes later, dark clouds showed up again, and all of a sudden, the rain and wind came back even harder than before.

I think that's kinda spooky, don't you? But you can see it for yourself when you make a mini-hurricane with this experiment!

Why did the sword swallower swallow an umbrella?
He wanted to put something away for a rainy day!

HERE'S THE STUFF YOU'LL NEED:

A large bowl

String

Scissors

1 small paper clip

Black pepper

A large spoon

Water

Ruler

READY, SET, SCIENCE!

STEP 1   Cut a piece of string about 6 inches (15 cm) long, using a ruler to help you. Tie one end of the string to the small paper clip. Cut off the extra bit of string. Pull gently on the paper clip to make it hang straight.

STEP 1

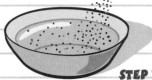

STEP 2   Fill the large bowl half full of water. Sprinkle pepper over the entire surface of the water.

STEP 2

STEP 3   Using the spoon, stir the water until it's going very fast. Watch what happens to the pepper. Record your observations in **RAPID DISASTER RESPONSE**.

STEP 3

STEP 4   Stir the water again until it's swirling very fast, same as in step 3. Then lower the paper clip into the center of the bowl until it's almost totally covered by the water. Try several times to find the exact center. Watch what happens to the paper clip, and record your observations and conclusion in **RAPID DISASTER RESPONSE**.

STEP 4

RAPID DISASTER RESPONSE

OBSERVATIONS

What happens to the pepper in **STEP 3**?

When you stir the water in **STEP 3**, does the pepper move faster on the outside or in the center?

What happens to the paper clip in **STEP 4** when it's in the exact center of the water?

CONCLUSION

Why do you think the paper clip in **STEP 4** doesn't move much when it's in the center of the water?

29

Keeping an Eye on the Eye of the Storm

Remember in Experiment 5: There She Blows! how spiraling wind moves the fastest? Well, in order for the wind to spiral, it has to whirl around a calm center area called the *eye*. When you stir the water, a calm area forms in the center of the whirling water, just like in the eye of a storm. Putting in the pepper helps you see the currents in the water. The pepper is carried by the currents, letting you see the way the wind and clouds spiral around the eye. In nature, these whirling winds come in the shape of a tornado funnel or the huge circular clouds of hurricanes.

Because of the rotation of the earth, these winds circle in a counter-clockwise direction in the northern hemisphere, while in the southern hemisphere the wind turns in a clockwise direction. When you stirred the water, did you make an American or Canadian hurricane (that is, did you stir the water counterclockwise), or did you make an Australian hurricane (did you stir the water clockwise)?

EXPERIMENT WITH THE EXPERIMENT 1: A HURRICANE HITS YOUR HOUSES (AND CARS, TOO)!

from your DISASTERS! KIT go grab:

- 2 mini houses
- 2 mini cars

HERE'S THE OTHER STUFF YOU'LL NEED:

The bowl with the water and the pepper from the first part of this experiment

The large spoon

What should you do when the eye of a hurricane passes?

Stay very still—maybe it won't see you!

READY, SET, SCIENCE!

Stir the water in the bowl to get it swirling really fast. Stop stirring, and drop a house into the water. Now drop the other house and the cars into the water. Watch what happens to the houses and cars, and record your observations in **RAPID DISASTER RESPONSE**.

RAPID DISASTER RESPONSE
OBSERVATIONS

Where do the houses and cars go: to the middle or the outside of the bowl?

Eye See What Happens to Houses and Cars!

In your experiment, the mini houses and cars should have been quickly forced toward the center of the bowl as they whirled around in the water. That's because the closer you get to the eye (at the center of the bowl), the faster the water moves. The houses and cars move closer and closer to the eye and whirl faster and faster, until they drop right into the eye. In the eye itself, the water is almost perfectly calm. If you watch closely, you'll see that after your houses and cars fall into the eye of your mini-hurricane, they hardly move. In a real hurricane you get the heaviest rains and winds right *around* the eye, up to 150 miles (240 km) per hour! But just a few feet or meters closer to the center, in the eye of the storm, there are only light breezes.

31

EXPERIMENT WITH THE EXPERIMENT 2: DOES SIZE MATTER?

The "eyes" have it!

HERE'S THE OTHER STUFF YOU'LL NEED:

A large glass

A large spoon

Water

Pepper

1 small paper clip

READY, SET, SCIENCE!

Now try the experiment again, this time in a large glass. Fill the glass two-thirds full with water, and sprinkle pepper on the surface. Use the spoon to stir the water until it's going very fast. A funnel should form in the center of the glass. Quickly lower the paper clip into the empty space in the center. That's the eye of the storm—as you know by now!

Why Size Matters!

When wind or water swirls in very tight circles, it moves even faster than when it goes in wider circles. Stirring the water in the glass makes the water move a lot faster than when you stir the water in the bowl. When you stir the water in the glass, the water goes so fast that it pushes against the glass and opens up a funnel down into the water that you can lower your paper clip into. The water swirling in the bowl is like a hurricane, and the water spinning in the glass is like a tornado. In nature, hurricanes can be hundreds of miles (or kilometers) wide, with wind speeds up to 150 miles (240 km) per hour. Tornadoes can reach a speed of 200 miles (320 km) per hour and are around 100 yards (90 m) wide!

#7: TERRIBLE TWISTERS

The other day I was playing soccer when a whirlwind came across the field. It picked up dried leaves and grass and swirled everything into the air. It was kinda neat to watch! But I know that whirlwinds are nothing compared to tornadoes—like the tornado that lifted Dorothy's house in _The Wizard of Oz!_ Now you can make your own mini-tornado with this experiment—wicked witches beware!

from your DISASTERS! KIT go grab:

Glitter
The washer
2 mini houses
2 mini cars

HERE'S THE OTHER STUFF YOU'LL NEED:

2 1-liter bottles (clear plastic soda bottles with labels removed)

Duct tape

Water

A friend (optional)

READY, SET, SCIENCE!

STEP 1   Fill one bottle about three-quarters full with water. Put the bottle down on a flat surface. Dump all of the glitter into the water.

STEP 2   Drop in the mini houses and cars.

STEP 3   Put the washer over the mouth of the bottle. Place the other empty bottle upside down on top of the washer so that the open mouths of the bottles are together.

STEP 3

STEP 4   Wrap the tape firmly around the necks of both bottles.

QUICK TIP

To avoid leaks, press on the tape to make sure it's sealed tightly against the bottles! You might need a friend to help you hold the bottles while you fasten the tape.

STEP 5   Carefully flip the bottles so the water-filled bottle is on top. Set it down on a flat surface, and quickly swirl the top bottle in a circular motion. What happens to the glitter and the mini houses and cars? Record your observations in *RAPID DISASTER RESPONSE*.

STEP 5

STEP 6   Flip the bottles over again. This time, swirl the water faster. When all the water has run out, flip the bottles over again. This time, swirl the water more slowly. Record your observations in *RAPID DISASTER RESPONSE*.

What goes around...
usually gets dizzy and
falls over!

RAPID DISASTER RESPONSE

OBSERVATIONS

What happens to the water as it leaves the top bottle in **STEP 5**?

Where does the glitter go in the whirling mass of water (which, by the way, is also known as a *vortex*) in **STEP 5**?

Where do the houses and cars go in **STEP 5**?

What happens in **STEP 6** when you swirl the water faster? When you swirl the water slower?

Getting to the Twisty Truth About Twisters

In this experiment, the way the water moves is kind of like the way air moves during a tornado. You can see the swirling currents more easily with the glitter in the water. The mini houses and cars also swirl around the funnel of air in the bottle because that's where the water is moving the fastest. The water moves downward in the bottle because of gravity, but in a tornado the wind currents move upward because of the lowered air pressure in the tornado's eye (which is, of course, at the center, as you know by now!).

Here's why the air pressure gets lowered: The winds are rotating so fast that they act like a mega vacuum cleaner, sucking the calm air out of the eye. The updraft of air's so strong, it can lift very heavy objects like trees and cars (or Dorothy's house) into the air! Sometimes people are carried miles away and are set down very gently. But if you're smart, you'll do your best to get underground *fast* when you see a tornado coming—'cause it's not likely to take you to Oz!

#8: FLASH FLOOD!

I hate getting wet! But water can do a lot more than just get my feathers damp. Every year, people all over the world lose their homes when a nearby river overflows its banks and floods the area. How much destruction can a flood cause? Build two mini towns in your backyard, and find out what happens to them when the water hits!

from your DISASTERS! KIT go grab:

- 3 tongue depressors
- 2 small wooden blocks
- 2 mini houses
- 2 mini cars

HERE'S THE OTHER STUFF YOU'LL NEED:

```
1 cookie sheet
1 cup
4 quarts (4.5 liters) of soil
Water
1 tablespoon
Glue
```

NOTE: Water and soil mixed together make mud! Since this experiment can get messy, it's best to do it outside. Place the cookie sheet on your driveway or patio where you can wash everything off later with a hose.

What is H2O?

You know! It's water.

Ok, then, what is H2O4?

It's 4 drinking!

READY, SET, SCIENCE!

STEP 1 Make a model of a river valley. You need to fill three-quarters of the cookie sheet with enough soil so that it can be mounded into a hill at one end. Moisten the soil with water and firmly press it into a sloping hill at least 5 inches (12 cm) high. The rest of the soil should gradually flatten out to approximately 1 inch (2.5 cm) high. It works better if the dirt slope makes little rolling hills on the way down from the big hill. Leave empty space at the other end of the cookie sheet so the water can run off. That can be your ocean!

STEP 2 Now you make a river! Use the spoon to gently carve a groove from the top of the hill down to the ocean at the other end. Try to go around some of the smaller hills. Pack the soil down tightly in the path of the river to make the water flow better.

STEP 3 Fill the cup halfway with water. Carefully pour the water on the hill so it flows into the path of the river you made. If the water doesn't go all the way to the ocean, lift up the end of the cookie sheet that has the hill on it. That will help push the water all the way through the river. Watch what happens to the river and the soil, and record your observations in *RAPID DISASTER RESPONSE.*

STEP 4 Carefully press the soil back into a hill, building it up where needed to adjust the path of your river. Remember, if you pack the soil tightly, the water will flow better through the river!

STEP 5 Use the mini houses and cars to create two "towns" along the river. Put one town on the hillside and the other closer to the ocean. If you want, you can add trees to your towns—get some twigs or grass, and stick them along the river and next to the houses.

STEP 5

STEP 6 To build a bridge across the river, place one wooden block on each side of the riverbed. Put a drop of glue on top of each block, and place one tongue depressor on the blocks. You can break the tongue depressor if the bridge needs to be shorter.

STEP 6

STEP 7 Use the other two tongue depressors to make a dam at the end of the stream just before it empties into the ocean. Break the tongue depressors in half, and stick the broken ends straight down into the soil, leaving the curving ends sticking up. Overlap them for additional strength, and pack down the soil around them. What do you think will happen *this* time when you pour the water? Record your hypotheses in **RAPID DISASTER RESPONSE**.

STEP 7

STEP 8 Fill the cup all the way up with water. Pour the water into the river, starting at the top of the hill. Let it flow for a few moments, then start pouring faster to force the water to go all the way down the path of the river. You can also lift up the end of the cookie sheet with the hill to help the river flow better. What happens *this* time? Record your observations in **RAPID DISASTER RESPONSE**.

RAPID DISASTER RESPONSE

OBSERVATIONS

Does the river in **STEP 3** flow through the groove you made in **STEP 2** or does it go somewhere else?

Does one end of the riverbed suffer more damage than the other?

HYPOTHESES

Do you think the dam you built in **STEP 7** will be able to keep the water from flowing into the ocean?

What will the water do to the bridges and towns?

OBSERVATIONS

What happens to the two towns during the flash flood in **STEP 8**?

Does your dam hold the water, or does it run into the ocean?

What has a mouth but no teeth?

A river!

A Flood of Facts

Floods cause incredible damage every year. Rivers usually flood because too much rain falls or because the snow melts too fast for the river to hold the runoff. When water rises higher, it spills over the riverbanks, causing a flood. Floods erode the land, cutting into the soil and carrying it away. A flood can also sweep away cars, trees, bridges, roads, and even houses!

I bet your model of a river valley looked very different after you poured water over it! The water makes deep cuts in your soil, in the same way that a flood erodes the land. Also, it probably got pretty swampy right underneath your soil hill; when there's a real flood, the land (called a *flood plain*) gets all covered in water, just like that.

When you caused your mini flood, the houses and the bridge in your towns were probably swept away. Houses on or near a flood plain really can be swept away or at least get pretty damaged when there's a flood. Your tongue depressor dam probably kept the water from running into your ocean for a little while. Most big rivers have dams built of concrete that can control flooding by blocking the water in a reservoir so it can be slowly released, giving people and crops enough water to last all year.

Knock, knock.

Who's there?

Wayne.

Wayne who?

Wayne drops keep falling on my head!

#9: AN EARTHSHAKING EXPERIENCE

I have something "earthshaking" to share with you! Did you know that you and your buds can make your own earthquake? Earthquakes are pretty major things, so it'll take you and two friends to do this experiment. The three of you will make a <u>seismograph</u> (an instrument that records the shaking of the earth) and see exactly what happens when the earth really moves!

HERE'S THE STUFF YOU'LL NEED:

An empty cereal box

A fat-tipped marker

A pencil

3 sheets of white paper

Scissors

Masking tape

A table or desk

2 friends

READY, SET, SCIENCE!

STEP 1 Cut the three sheets of white paper in half lengthwise. Now you have six narrow sheets of paper. Use the masking tape to tape the ends of these six narrow sheets together to make one long strip. That's your seismograph paper.

STEP 2 Using the scissors, carefully cut four slits in the front of a cereal box. Two of the slits should be near the top and two near the bottom. Each pair of slits should be about 1 inch (2.5 cm) apart from each other. Make sure these slits are at least 5 inches (12 cm) long, so the strip of paper can slide through.

STEP 2

STEP 3 Feed the paper strip through the bottom two slits, first down into the box, then back out. Then pull the strip up to the top two slits, feed it down into the box, and then back out.

STEP 3

STEP 4 Close the box and tape it shut. Then use the masking tape to keep the box on the desk or table. Make sure you don't tape down the paper! It needs to slide freely through the slits.

STEP 4

STEP 5 Here's where you need your two pals. You face the box on the table, steadily holding the fat marker so the tip touches the paper on the cereal box. Pal #1 stands to your left, at the end of the table, and slowly pulls the paper so it slides through the slits in the box. Pal #2 stands to your right, directly across from Pal #1, and shakes the table from side to side, gently at first, and then building up to big shakes. Then slow back down to gentle shaking before building up to big shakes again. Pal #2 does this as many times as he or she can.

STEP 6 When the strip of paper pulls all the way through, all of you can stop. Take the strip of paper and lay it flat on the table to examine it. Circle the bigger line marks with a pencil. Record your observations and conclusion in *RAPID DISASTER RESPONSE.*

Giving Earthquakes a Fair Shake

The shaking of the table is supposed to be kind of like the shaking of the earth during an earthquake. It took energy from Pal #2 to shake the table, and it takes energy to shake the ground during an earthquake!

Where does that energy come from? Well, the ground you walk on isn't as solid as it seems! Earth's surface is divided into giant plates of solid rock floating on molten rock (like the stuff in volcanoes). When two of these plates smack into each other, that can cause an earthquake!

One of the ways we measure how much the earth is shaking is with the seismograph. When the ground shakes a lot, the pen in a real seismograph moves more than when it only shakes a little. When Pal #2 shook the table a lot, I bet you got bigger markings on your seismograph paper (called a *seismogram*) than when Pal #2 only shook the table a little bit.

43

#10: EARTHQUAKE SURVIVAL STRUCTURE

Have you ever been in an earthquake? I have, and boy, is it weird! The floor sort of moves and shakes underneath you, and things like the curtains and the stuff on the bookshelves start moving. In a really bad earthquake, houses can fall down! That's why in places that get lots of earthquakes, like San Francisco, the buildings are designed to stand up against tough quakes. What's so special about these buildings? Build your own earthquake survival structure, and find out!

HERE'S THE STUFF YOU'LL NEED:

13 mini marshmallows

32 toothpicks

1 hardcover book
(250-350 pages long)

READY, SET, SCIENCE!

QUICK TIP

To make your structure strong enough to withstand an earthquake, be sure to poke the toothpick all the way through the marshmallow until the pointy tip is sticking out!

STEP 1   To make your earthquake-proof building, start with four toothpicks and four marshmallows to form a square. Stick the first toothpick into the first marshmallow until the pointy tip pokes out the other side. To the other end of that first tooth-pick, stick on the second marshmallow until the pointy end comes out. Then stick two other toothpicks into each of those marshmallows at right angles. Stick a marshmallow onto the open ends of these two toothpicks (that's a total of two more marshmallows). Connect these last two marshmallows with the fourth toothpick, forming a square.

STEP 1

STEP 2   Now, add eight more toothpicks and five more marshmallows to enlarge that square into a grid of four connected squares. Overlap the toothpicks as you stick them through the marshmallows in the first square.

STEP 2

STEP 3   Now turn the four connected squares into four connected pyramids. First, take four toothpicks and stick each one straight down into each of the four marshmallows at the corners of the first square. Gently squeeze all four toothpicks toward the center of the first square, and join them together with one marshmallow. Repeat this with the other three squares in the grid, adding the four remaining marshmallows.

STEP 3a

STEP 3b

EXPERIMENT CONTINUES ON THE NEXT PAGE!

STEP 4 Finish the structure by joining the marshmallows at the top of the four pyramids with the last four toothpicks to form a square.

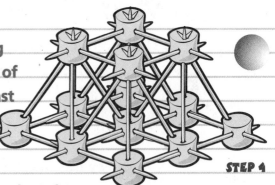
STEP 4

STEP 5 You now have an excellent earthquake-proof building—or do you? Time to put it to the test! Place the building on a table. Go grab the book and carefully put it on top of your building.

STEP 6 When you have the book balanced on your building, start shaking the table. Do it softly at first, and watch what happens to the building and the book. Keep shaking harder, and see what happens. Record your observations and conclusion in **RAPID DISASTER RESPONSE.**

RAPID DISASTER RESPONSE

OBSERVATIONS
What happens to your building and the book on top of it when you shake the table in **STEP 6**?

Is your building strong enough to withstand the softer shaking?

What happens when you shake the table harder in **STEP 6**?

CONCLUSION
What can happen to real buildings during an earthquake?

Earthquake Survival Sense

Buildings collapse during earthquakes if their supports aren't strong enough or if their supports are too rigid. That's why you used marshmallows as cement; they are flexible and act as shock absorbers. Your building and book sway but remain standing in spite of the gentle shaking. The building also needs to be strong, so that's why you poke the toothpicks all the way through the marshmallows, to make sure they overlap. That gives your building some firm support. But even the strongest structures can collapse, like yours probably did, if they're shaken hard enough!

Most injuries during earthquakes are caused by collapsing buildings and falling objects. The most important thing is knowing how to protect yourself during an earthquake. Don't run into the street, or you could be hit by falling bricks and debris! The best thing to do if you feel the floor start to shake is to duck and take cover under a sturdy table or desk, and wait until the earthquake stops.

What happened to the boat in the middle of an earthquake?

It became a nervous wreck!

SNEAK PEEK PUZZLE

So that's it for this workbook of disaster experiments! Want a hint about what kind of science we'll be exploring next month? Just solve this puzzle to find out. Fill in the blanks for the 10 questions below. Then put the numbered letters in order, and you'll have the answer. Check to see if you're right at the bottom of the page. Until I see you again—steer clear of disasters!

1 When a meteorite hits, it forms a crater and ___ ___ ___ ___.
                                         3

2 The calm center of a hurricane is called the eye of the ___ ___ ___ ___ ___.
                                              1

3 Your volcano erupts because you make a chemical
___ ___ ___ ___ ___ ___ ___ ___.
                       6

4 The quickest way for wind to travel is for it to ___ ___ ___ ___ ___ ___.
                                       4

5 A large mass of rock or snow that moves quickly down a mountain slope is an
___ ___ ___ ___ ___ ___ ___ ___ ___.
                      5

6 A seismograph records the energy of
___ ___ ___ ___ ___ ___ ___ ___ ___ ___.
 10

7 A whirling mass of water or air is a ___ ___ ___ ___ ___ ___.
                              7

8 In the Live Lava experiment, the ___ ___ ___ ___ ___ was first to reach a mini house on your cookie sheet.
                                     2

9 During an earthquake, you should duck and take
___ ___ ___ ___ ___.
 9

10 A funnel cloud about 100 yards (90 m) wide with winds at 200 mph (320 kph) is a
___ ___ ___ ___ ___ ___ ___.
               8

Here's what we'll be doing next month:

___ ___ ___ ___ ___ ___ ___ ___ ___ ___!
 1   **2**   **3**   **4**   **5**   **6**   **7**   **8**   **9** **10**

48